VILLA JULIE COLLEGE LIBRARY
STEVENSON, MD 21153

VEIL

NEW AND SELECTED POEMS

Rae Armantrout

WESLEYAN UNIVERSITY PRESS

MIDDLETOWN, CONNECTICUT

Published by Wesleyan University Press, Middletown, CT 06459

© 2001 by Rae Armantrout

All rights reserved

Printed in the United States of America

5 4 3 2 1

Library of Congress Cataloging-in-Publication Data

Armantrout, Rae, 1947–
   Veil : new and selected poems / Rae Armantrout.
     p. cm.
   ISBN 0-8195-6449-4 (cloth : alk. paper)—ISBN
   0-8195-6450-8 (paper : alk. paper)
     I. Title
   PS3551.R455 V45 2001
   811'.54dc21   2001002578

Acknowledgments

Some of the poems in *Veil* first appeared in the following journals:
American Poetry Review, The Electronic Review, Fence, New American Writing, The Southern Review (Australia), *Talisman, The Germ, Sulfur.*
"Words" appeared in an anthology called *POG 1* (co-published by POG and Chax in 1999, ed. Charles Alexander). *Extremities,* The Figures, 1978, *The Invention of Hunger,* Tuumba, 1979, *Precedence,* Burning Deck, 1985, Rae Armantrout, *Necromance* (Los Angeles: Sun & Moon Press, 1991) pp. 7–8, 10, 11, 24, 29, 39, 41, 43, 47. ©1991 by Rae Armantrout. Reprinted by permission of Sun & Moon Press. Rae Armantrout, *Made to Seem* (Los Angeles: Sun & Moon Press, 1995) pp. 11, 13, 16, 21, 29, 33, 42, 53, 57). ©1995 by Rae Armantrout. Reprinted by permission of Sun & Moon Press. Rae Armantrout, *The Pretext* (Los Angeles: Green Integer, forthcoming) ©2000 by Rae Armantrout. Reprinted by permission of Green Integer. Four poems from *The Pretext* were published in a chapbook writing the plot about sets, Chax, 1998. "Engines" ©1983, 1992 by Rae Armantrout & Ron Silliman previously appeared in *Conjunctions 4* and in *Demo to Ink.*

Contents

VEIL

Foreword

"Aloha, Fruity Pebbles": The Poems of Rae Armantrout

RON SILLIMAN

For some years the largest gathering of the poetry of Rae Armantrout was in French, a selection translated "de l'américain" by Denis Dormoy in 1991 for the Cahiers de Royaumont series under the title Couverture. When Made to Seem eclipsed that volume, it did so by exactly one page, 58 for its 31 poems to Couverture's 57 pages, 21 texts. At 73 poems—roughly one-quarter of her life's work dating back to 1970—Veil presents us with not merely the richest and most panoramic view we have been given of her poetry to date, but also a particularly dense reading experience, given just how many of these texts at first appear utterly straightforward.

In this sense, Armantrout belongs to what might be characterized as the literature of the vertical anti-lyric, those poems that at first glance appear contained and perhaps even simple, but which upon the slightest examination rapidly provoke a sort of vertigo effect as element after element begins to spin wildly toward more radical (and, often enough, sinister) possibilities. Armantrout's ancestors in this are not so much Lorine Niedecker, with whom she has been compared more than once, nor her teachers such as Denise Levertov, but rather Jack Spicer, Emily Dickinson, and Arthur Rimbaud.

It is as pointless to characterize Armantrout's writing as surreal as it is to identify it as an instance of language writing. Nowhere else in either tendency is there anything quite like these works. If they are often disturbing in their subtextual resonances, these poems are also remarkably cheerful and good-natured, written with an ear for (and eye to) American popular culture that is the most acute in contemporary poetry. Imagine David Lynch as rewritten by Frank O'Hara and you'll be somewhere in the ballpark, except that Armantrout's work lacks the claustrophobic mannerism of the former and the casualness (feigned or otherwise) of the latter.

Anxiety seems to be an initial impulse motivating many of these poems. What the poems don't do, ever, is to propose resolution. In this, they're directly opposed to the vignette school of suburban verse. Often, in fact, we end far more tightly wound up than when we began. At the same time, we're exhilarated at all the connections we've made along the way, and by how much more filled in this sense of what's bothering us has become in the course of a few stanzas.

Some of this wired feeling Armantrout achieves through the brilliantly worked finish her poems have, a polish that often combines with her sense of pop culture to give phrases, stanzas, entire pieces an air of "rightness" that can make them appear timeless, as though the poems were simply waiting to have been written. Consider the first section of "Manufacturing," one of Armantrout's more recent works:

A career in vestige management.

A dream job
back-engineering
shifts in salience.

I'm so far
behind the curve
on this.

So. Cal.
must connect with
so-called

to manufacture
the present.

Ubiquity's
the new in-joke

bar-code hard-on,

a catch-phrase
in every segment.

How it might be possible to improve on this particular machine made of words, I'm at a loss to imagine. What is being constructed in "Manufacturing" is not reality so much as meaning management, whose relationship to the noticeably uncertain and isolated speaker is distant and must be as cynical in its mode of production as it appears in its reception. The punning use of "dream" and connotative fields cast by "vestige management," "back-engineering," and "salience" thrust the literal abstraction hidden within "behind the curve" toward the reader with a searing poignancy, as if Armantrout has been able to peel back the figurative manifestation of longing to unveil the emotion itself. The point is driven home when it then focuses on the simple immanence of an otherwise unnamed "this."

By tucking the sole complete verb thus far in "Manufacturing" under the apostrophe of "I'm," the verb phrase of the fourth stanza jumps out to balance the deliciously ironic equation of "So. Cal."—pronounced exactly as it's spelled—with "so-called," an adjective standing in here for the unnameable noun. The next stanza, which is in fact the predicate of a predicate phrase, is the closest thing you will find in Armantrout's poetry to an actual topic sentence. This is followed immediately with a joke about a joke, a paradox whose impossibility is precisely its point. Again the verb (the last one we will get in this section) is tucked under an apostrophe.

The next line—*bar-code hard-on*—leaps out not only because it is the first since the poem's beginning to be isolated on its own stanza, but also due to its paratactic relation to what appears to have been the first part of this sentence. The riveting near parallelism of the vowel sequence (the tonal difference of the "o" between "code" and "on" signaling a shift without giving away *what of*) heightens the clash between commerce and the erotic.

One of those lines, having once read it, you will never forget, *bar-code hard-on* figures an instant of utter intensity, a signature feature of Armantrout's writing. No poet since Lew Welch could have imagined that prosody—yet it seems absolutely self-evident—and no poet other than Armantrout could have joined those words in that fashion.

Any other poet would have closed the section—and perhaps the poem—right there. It's characteristic of Armantrout that she doesn't. Having arrived at this moment, the poem turns hard on that line's terminal comma to give the text one harsh last twist. Harking back to the Depression-era political promise of a chicken in every pot, "a catch-phrase / in every segment" functions instead as a threat—there will be no aspect of the real that has not already been vetted through the process of marketing, a logo stuck on every apple, even the plastic separator that consumers drop onto the checkout stand's miniaturized conveyor belt understood as a space to be sold. Marketing is all that is the case. In the same instant as this vision of totalitarian capital, the last stanza looks back at its immediate predecessor as if to question its own complicity in this process. Are the values that make good writing good—complexity, concision, an "ear"—themselves part of the problem? This poem is going to let neither the writer nor the reader off the hook.

Perhaps what is most remarkable about the first section of "Manufacturing" is that on June 21, 1998, just five days before this version was finalized, it was the initial section of a poem then called "Veer":

> My career in vestige management.
>
> My dream job back-engineering
> shifts in salience

to resemble the wind
by channel flipping.

I set maternal function
at deep tissue
interference pattern
caresses.

In the dream, I tell an incredulous
directory assistance operator
that robbers have taken
my phone service. I need the address
of the Paradise Valley Branch
which was so helpful before.
She thinks I'm kidding her.

Wake up
and you become that operator.

Now "a pall
of suspicion hangs
over the investigations."

Among the language poets, Armantrout is perhaps the most rigorous and obsessive reviser—revision in some vital inner-driven sense is her process of writing. For years, she has sent versions and revisions of poems to a small and somewhat rotating cluster of friends, notably including Fanny Howe, Bob Perelman, Steve Benson, Lyn Hejinian, and Lydia Davis, a privileged if informal group that I've been a part of for three decades. Since the advent of the Internet, drafts and revisions even of a single line can and occasionally do travel back and forth several times in one day. It has never been evident to me precisely how Armantrout uses her focus-group feedback—the responses often directly contradict one another and the writing processes of these poets are quite different from one another. It is, I suspect, more important to Armantrout as a part of her thinking through of the text to have each line examined from several alternate perspectives than it may be for the literal input any one of her peers might offer.

This earlier version includes the administered realm of marketing's dystopia at the far end of "channel flipping," but it seems a minor point of what is presented as a dream narrative. The focus of the first draft focuses not on the constructed surface of a ubiquitous real, but rather upon the speaker herself, figured here as a mother and shifting noticeably in the next-to-final stanza from the first person into an even more intimate second. Of the eight shifters (*my, I, you, she*) of the first version, only one survives—though it is none of the ones from the initial draft—in the final edit. The text is in this sense far less personal. Evidence of other people has literally been deleted. But the result is an experience far more interior for its sense of objectness. The final version is written right on the membrane betwixt self and other. As the poems from which Armantrout's 1979 book *The Invention of Hunger* takes its name[1] puts it:

> Discomfort marks the boundary

> One early symptom was the boundary.

In "Manufacturing," nature is already hopelessly stained with this all-but-invisible film of culture. One of Armantrout's earliest poems appears to declare the problem at the top of its lungs:

> VIEW

> Not the city lights. We want

> -the moon-

> The Moon

> none of our own doing!

Although I have read this poem hundreds of times over more than 25 years, what never goes away from this seemingly blunt assertion is the absolute strangeness of Armantrout's

---

1. The poem itself has what for Armantrout is a heavily coded title: "Natural History."

punctuation. The moon is repeated, as though flickering. It never appears as itself, but bracketed between these very curious dashes or with the most lurid of capitals. The poem's final line is a sentence that has no beginning: the desire it articulates did not begin with us.

William Carlos Williams once thought to show readers how to get the facticity of "a red wheel / barrow // glazed with rain / water // beside the white / chickens" into a poem. Again and again, Armantrout's texts unveil the framing device itself: So much depends in fact upon Williams's initial phrase—"so much depends / upon"—that the implements and animals must always remain perpetually out of reach. It is not possible to step outside of this fatal equation ("Ubiquity's / the new in-joke"). In Armantrout's Oz, you can never ignore the man behind the curtain.

These poems return obsessively to this Wittgensteinian double bind: The objects and events of this world can never be experienced directly, absent all mediation. Yet the details that Armantrout provides for this profound conundrum offer the most American and even sweet traps imaginable, made all the more excruciating by their friendliness, masked not as despair so much as Natalie Wood, Daffy, or Goofy:

> "Well, look who missed
> the fleeting moment,"
>
> Green Giant gloats
> over dazed children.
>
> > "Covers"

*

> That young girl listening
> to "Angel Baby"
>
> on a pink plastic radio
> while staring out her window
> at the planet Venus
>
> > "Near Rhyme"

> Pigeons bathe in technicolor
> fluid "of a morning"
>
> "Confidential"

As this last poem cited underscores, the peculiar fate of the American world may be that the most serious questions can only be posed through the vocabulary of U.S. culture, which infantilizes everything it touches:

> If I was banging
> my head with a shoe,
> I was just exaggerating—
>
> like raising my voice
> or the ante.
>
> Curlicues
> on iron gratings:
>
> Can it be
> a flourish is a grimace
> but a grimace isn't a flourish?

"'Aloha, Fruity Pebbles!'" rings out "On the inscribed surface / of sleep"—never a blank slate in Armantrout's dreamworld—but we never get to know why exactly. Here the commercial for a children's cereal becomes what the sirens sing to sailors: "Almost constant / bird soundings." Longing for the unmediated, we find only pigeons in paradise, crooning to us in the familiar refrains of daytime TV. Passages of this sort, which are everywhere throughout Veil, carry their own sound track:

> Music, useful
> for abstracting emphasis:
>
> Sweet nothing
> to do with me.

Paoli, Pennsylvania
March 2000

from

Extremities

EXTREMITIES

Going to the Desert
is the old term

"landscape of zeroes"

the glitter of edges
again catches the eye

to approach these swords!

lines across which
beings vanish / flare

the charmed verges of presence

GRACE

1

a spring there
where his entry must be made

signals him on

2

the sentence
           flies

isn't turned to salt
no stuttering

3

I am walking

covey in sudden flight

GENERATION

We know the story.

She turns
back to find her trail
devoured by birds.

The years; the
undergrowth

TONE

I

Hoping my face shows the pleasure I felt, I'm
smiling languidly. Acting. To put your mind
at rest—how odd! At first we loved because
we startled one another

2

    Not pleased to see the
    rubber band, chapstick, tin-
    foil, this pen, things
    made for our use

    But the bouquet you made
    of doorknobs, long nails for
    their stems   sometimes
    brings happiness

3

Is it bourgeois to dwell on nuance? Or effeminate?
Or should we attend to it the way a careful animal
sniffs the wind?

4

    Say the tone of an afternoon

    Kindly but sad

    "The ark of the ache of it"

    12 doorsteps per block

5

In the suburbs butterflies
still spiral up the breeze
like a drawing of weightlessness.
To enter into this spirit!
But Mama's saying she's alright
"as far as breathing and all that"

6

When you're late I turn slavish, listen hard for
your footstep. Sound that represents the end of
lack

VIEW

Not the city lights. We want

-the moon-

The Moon
none of our own doing!

XENOPHOBIA

I

"must represent the governess
for, of course, the creature itself
could not inspire such terror."

staring at me fixedly, no
trace of recognition.

"when the window opened of its own accord.
In the big walnut tree
were six or seven wolves . . .

strained attention. They were white."

(The fear of cloudy skies.)

like strangers! After five years

Misgiving. Misdoubt.

2

(The fear that one is dreaming.)

The moon was shining, suddenly
everything around me appeared
(The fear of)
unfamiliar.

Wild vista
inside or near the home.

(Dread of bearing a monster.)

If I failed to overlook
the torn cushions,

three teapots side by side,
strewn towels, socks, papers—

both foreign and stale.

3

when I saw the frame was rotten,
crumbling away from the glass,
in spots, in other places still attached
with huge globs of putty.

The doctor forced me to repeat the word.

Chimera. Cold feet.

scared and unreal looking at buildings.
The thin Victorians with scaly paint,
their flimsy backporches linked
by skeletal stairways.

4

After five years
(The fear that you are not at home.)

I was sitting in the alcove where I never sit
when I noticed a single eye,

crudely drawn in pencil,
in a corner near the floor.

The paint was blistering—
beneath it I saw white.

5

Sparrows settle on the sagging wires.

(Fear of sights not turned to words.)

Horrific. Grisly.
"Rumplestiltskin!"

Not *my* expression.

Not my net of veins
beneath thin skin.

(A morbid dread of throbbing.)

Of its own accord

ANTI-SHORT STORY

A girl is running. *Don't* tell me
"She's running for her bus."

All that aside!

from

The Invention
of Hunger

NATURAL HISTORY

1

Discomfort marks the boundary.

One early symptom was the boundary.

The invention of hunger.
I could *use* energy.

To serve.

Elaborate systems in the service of
far-fetched demands.

The great termite mounds serve
as air-conditioners.

Temperature within must never vary
more than 2 degrees.

2

Which came first
the need or the system?

Systematic.
System player.
Scheme of Things.

The body considered as a functional unit.
"My system craves calcium."

An organized set of doctrines.

A network formed for the purpose of . . .

"All I want is you."

3

was narrowing their options to one,
the next development.

Soldiers have elongate heads and massive mandibles.
Squirtgun heads are found among fiercer species.
Since soldiers cannot feed themselves, each requires
a troupe of attendants.

4

Her demands had become more elaborate.

He must be blindfolded,
    (Must break off his own wings)
wear this corset laced tight
    (seal up the nuptial cell)
to attain his heart's desire.

Move only as she permits
    (Mate the bloated queen each season)
or be hung from the rafters.
How did he get here?

5

Poor baby,
I heard your hammer.

The invention of pounding.

"As soon as it became important
that free energy be channeled."

Once you cared to be
set off
from the surrounding medium.

This order has been preferred
since improvement was discovered.

The moment one intends to grow
at the expense.

When teeth emerge

Demand for special treatment
was an early symptom

FICTION

When the woman's face contorted and she clutched the railing for support, we knew she would die for this was a film with the set trajectory of fiction.

*

When she looked down at the birthmark on her leg, it did not seem out of place like a blemish. Rather like a landmark on a loved terrain. She had always answered "no" with a touch of indignation when people asked if she had burned herself. But when she saw her bare leg in the mirror, the red splotch surprised her. From the alien perspective, it appeared extraneous

*

The measure of fear is the distance between an event and its mental representation. Small doses were sometimes taken for pleasure. Distortion locked in the funhouse and tickets sold.

*

Her month old son would really watch her now, she hoped. After three days she should seem "strangely familiar."

*

The old architecture.

Roof over
the tongue

Hands wandering netherworlds. A sense of self starts in the mouth and spreads slowly.

pacifier. Lost again and
crying because empty.

"He's just a baby."
"He's just hungry."
"He's just scared."

The poor vacuum!
as best he can

Her elderly father said the baby looked "like a wise little old man."

He predicted her child would be male. His motive was obvious. He insisted this baby would look Irish as he did—himself reborn in a form she must love. She hated such transparency. "When have your hunches paid off before?" she asked. She planned to give birth to a girl who resembled her husband's family or perhaps no one at all. An utterly new countenance. When a grandson was born who did resemble him, her erstwhile hostile father grew doting. A superstitious streak she fought against made it difficult not to accept the prophecy entirely now, with all its implications.

*

Furthering the story.
Furthering
'the ends of the species'

*

Driving imitated sanity.
Blurred gargoyles shrank into the past.
Why should she notice or care?

*

When her husband was late, she imagined him dead. Now that
he had a son, she feared, he could be killed on the highway.

*

"Everything's a message," her friend said. And her son's birth
injury must be a sign, symbol of some weakness in her think-
ing or her life.

*

crying because lost. The growing
fibers of desire cannot
locate . . .

*

Fuss Balloon. Squirm Bag. The hero's nicknames described un-
expected animation.

In the Bach fugue it was difficult to know which theme was the traveler with whom one should identify. One's self.

*

In his old age he went mad. Any stress, including the imminent operation, returned him to an incident that occurred during WWII. The "Japs" had torpedoed his ship and it had almost sunk. Now, whenever he got agitated, he would yell, "We're taking on water." This idea was like a painted screen let down between himself and the particulars of his danger.

*

The French reserve a special past tense for fictions.

*

She seemed to enjoy each new crisis as if it were a complication in the plot of a comedy, a mere detour en route to the happy resolution she was still expecting 'after this'
   old 'after this'   dear 'after this'

DUSK

spider on the cold expanse
of glass, three stories high
rests intently
and so purely alone.

I'm not like that!

from
Precedence

DOUBLE

So these are the hills of home. Hazy tiers
nearly subliminal. To see them is to see
double, hear bad puns delivered with a wink.
An untoward familiarity.

Rising from my sleep, the road is more
and less the road. Around that bend are pale
houses, pairs of junipers. Then to *look*
reveals no more.

POSTCARDS

Man in
the eye clinic
rubbing his
eye—

too convincing. Like
memory.

My parents' neighbors' house,
backlit,
at the end of their street.

SINGLE MOST

Leaves fritter.

Teased edges.

It's vacillation that pleases.

Who answers for
the "whole being"?

This is
only the firing.

*

Daffy runs along
the synapses, hooting
in mock terror.

Then he's shown
on an embankment, watching
the noisy impulse pass.

*

But there's always a steady hum
shaped like a room
whose door must lead to
what really

where "really"
is a nervous
tic as regular

*

as as   as as

the corner repeats itself

*

Dull frond:
giant lizard tongue
stuck out
in the murky distance
sight slides off
as a tiny elf.

*

Patients are asked to picture
health as an unobstructed
hall or tube
through which Goofy now tumbles:
Dumb luck!

Unimagined
creature scans postcard.

*

Conclusions can be drawn.

Shadows add depth
by falling

while deep secrets
are superseded—

quaint.

Exhaling
on second thought

TRAVELING THROUGH THE YARD

(For William Stafford)

It was lying near my back porch
in the gaudy light of morning—
a dove corpse, oddly featherless,
alive with flies.
I stopped,
dustpan in hand, and heard
them purr over their feast.
To leave that there would make some stink!
So thinking hard for all of us,
I scooped it up, heaved it
across the marriage counselor's fence.

ADMISSION

The eye roves,
back and forth, as
indictment catches up?

If shadows tattoo
the bare shelf,
they enter by comparison?

A child's turntable fastened
to the wall with a white cord
will not?

Unless on its
metal core
an unspeakable radiance . . .

Think in order
to recall
what the striking thing

resembles.
(So impotently
loved the world

THROUGH WALLS

Stomach: lonely.

Curled up in the
familiar ring,
she went to sleep.

What a world, little churl!

Raw grass blades and
these spearheaded weeds,
disheveled.

                Sun glancing.

Heat
did not
come home

to whom?

As if porous . . .
                Passing through

*

Hungry for a garden's
whispered care.

Those blues and pinks.

                          Who has
            saved some for you

may part
the afternoon from an evening
looked to and
looking back
or down on our
walled off suspense.

"There's more," we are
to understand.

Excreting one more
link, and putting
a leaf back
on either side, a fin, a stroke, this
slow progress.

                    *

The awful thing
if every spurt
left him—

Anonymous Phrase—

in here   and there it
surfaces
under the hidden eyes of
Brer Fox and Brer Bear.

"Nana, na, nana."

*

Ready tongue.

Coming back at
her sister, then
willing
to address the world's
intelligent and
uninhabited designs.

Most at home when
well-known
words come through
the metal
wires, the unseen
"transformers"
                saying
". . . reminds me of my home
far away."

FICTION

Excitement of being someone else about whom
a remark was imagined dominated her morning.

Being young, he drew weather and taped it
on the walls.

Everywhere posed scenes solicited explanation.

The bumper-sticker on the white pick-up read
"Alien."

It was exhausting and provocative.

One might have admired a work composed
of such obscure and equivocal elements
for its durability.

But believing was eating, day by day, the long
extraneous fibers and swallowing fast.

Swollen kindness and cruelty could be seen
from a great distance.

Children grew from our exaggerations.

The new television perched upon the console
of the old.

A ballerina fluttered on toe before a hammer
and sickle.

(What did the bitter, green nodules say to
the smeared glass?)

A Black man in a Union-Jack t-shirt was
yelling, "Do you have any idea what I mean?"

PRECEDENCE

The dead boy
was found
clasping, "wrapped around"
a tree,
one chosen in a
roiling wilderness,
the urgent dream
where love gives way to rescue.
Or rescue to love

HOME FEDERAL

A merchant is
probing for us
with his chintz curtain

                    effect.

          *

"Ha, ha, you missed me,"
a dead person says.

          *

There's the bank's
colonial balcony
where no one has

                    ever stood.

Engines

Rae Armantrout and Ron Silliman

A herd of wild helicopters scuds in the night. Syllabics penetrate the red mulch of values, skeletons bloom at the rear of the lab so recently repainted a pale green. Fingers curl slowly in sleep. The logic of ambition is to seem a straight line. In the butcher shops of the North End blood stains the flesh of skinned rabbits. Style is its own mark. Electrical storms in the skull cloud the eye. The volley maintained nears orgasm. Narcs prefer down vests, the low cut in the rear concealing both gun and handcuffs. The smell of curry in the corridor of the small hotel. You stand in the glass booth, pretending conversation. Under the back stairs cobwebs define the spiders' hunt. The noise of the fan cooling the slide projector is punctuated with clicks. The cosmos is a purple flower.

Unable to reply, melodrama skips ahead. "I think something happens in the end." Her face, like her mother's, is tense. One death had sent an unidentifiable pulse of dread across three unborn generations. "How will I know when I make a mistake?" Pinpointing errors, I know where I am. A yellow "sea" or "field" of vinyl tufts. Glamor makes sense of the creature. So they laid her in a glass coffin. The spirits whom we call angels were never at any time or in any way darkness. The eucalyptus only seems to shrug. Light flicks over those leaves in complete silence. That is a slippery tongue. Do we suggest relations we aren't willing to declare?

For this paragraph, attach separate form 1040-ES. His face, like his mother's, was dense. Instinctively we crouched, disembarking the Sikorsky, darting swiftly in a bent-over manner beyond the wide sweep of the blade (which only became visible as it slowed to a stop). The red spot on the beak of the male gull is thought "beautiful." Her one idea provokes disaster. He came in from behind. There are several ways in which this can be taken, but we prefer air freight. In a magazine, store ammo. The body distills poisons. Something longer and more languid perhaps, convoluted, looking simultaneously over its shoulder and between its legs, saddened by the very idea of girth, wearing a saxophone like a medal or sunglasses after dark. I chance this sentence at the point of max conflict. Thank you Saint Jude. Over several months he domesticated the rat, making a pet of it. Melodrama *skips?*

Skeletons *bloom?* Animated by a sense of unreality and a love of measurement. It needs to be shown that no mistake is possible. A radio projects an arc of interlocking squares onto the otherwise soft morning. He attempts a series of irrefutable statements. "An angel equals his traits. Vertical red lines distinguish the horsefly's snout. What anybody might call head." Unsure where the danger ends, we remain crouched. It is more difficult to believe that the holy angels are now unaware of their eternal blessedness. Playing the lecher, someone strikes a simple pose and thus hopes to escape notice. We are happy to leave the beach, begin a segmented evening. So accustomed am I to spinning that reappearance seems a moral good. Maybe waggling leaves won't work.

But a fern is not intended. This is a redo. The metaphor of person lurks in the work. Great numerical hysteria is numbed by words. The angel was not as we had expected, but moody and violent. Bats weep in the shadows of the foundry. He found hair flattened to the leg by the scrim of nylon intensely erotic. Number makes the simple marriage. The radio speaks to the kitchen. 66. Huge, well-hung, balls of type. We putter about the desert. The large child disassembled the crib. They take on the countenance of helicopters, shuttling from the clouds.

For the sake of argument, one point has been elevated. A pinhead. Often invoked, seldom identified. Hi, Mom. After a "peak experience" the poor monster dies happy. I won't die, for then I wouldn't grow in your enlarging appraisal. Pleasure detaches from the stroke and spreads. I recognize the soft jolt as a car door closing in the street. In heaven it would not arise. One grows more individual—uniquely marred and indescribably attired, unable to join the talk. You must be the angel, Gabriel. You must be the color red. I wanted each sentence to leave a question in mind—a sense of puzzlement—vague, at first, but capable of being formulated. Pressure fills the channel nicely, not exactly wet.

More gentle than the art of pushing is the desire slowly to withdraw. The head is both swollen and mottled. The angel steps under a streetlamp to light a cigarette. Only the policemen's horses appear neutral to the sight of so much blood. The next slide is of an invoice. Their wings are like blades. This is inserted to test your response. It has the look and feel of milky eggwhite. Thanksgiving is marked by a fire at the hotel. His fear was of scale. By themselves, they are silent. The unit for gum is the stick. You must be the window. The clouds go red at twilight.

You are the void from which the angels create the archangels. The massless particle created in Beta decay is not, in fact, the neutrino. The semblance of existence lurks in the verb. A group is a band or host. Sustained in euphoria by the statements of their clothes. Dialogue excuses the creature. Pearls perch on crinkled lobes. At daybreak the old palm looks reptilian. Razor backed, then sabertoothed. Though a burning log does form a *strange* landscape, nothing that glows can be called desolate. Metatron is called the scribe of heaven. Recorded song refers to dreams. This blasted backlot is of no account. Then she caught sight of something not exhausted by its name.

A helicopter. Style is the fiber in description which shrinks at the first wash. His argument that flight was discontinuous only made them more nervous, stare more intently at the three-panel, four-color plastic *Emergency* instructions, whose universality was marked by the total lack of text. The angels stand in front of the cabin and indicate how to place the mask against your face, in the event it "drops" from a compartment next to the irritating jets of air. I stood on the beach of a small island, watching all of that pass from the surface. Narrative suppresses immediate attention. The sky is blue by agreement, however not today. The collie howling over the figure of the fallen settler in the snow is frozen on the wall of my grandmother's diningroom, which does not exist. The opposite of memory is nostalgia. An old billiard table is no longer an exact surface. Blood gels on the instant of contact. Take a deep breath. Some conversation is not a come-on. I mean: *stampedes* in the night.

Static emblems in the train of thought. In America we are wistful about horses. The plural is restful and suggestive. Unwilling to surrender their role, the congratulatory party went to photograph the encased newborn surrounded by monitors. Is there an exact instance? Is she the lady of the house? Light bounds toward her drugged eyes unparried (unparalleled). Out there gigantic fronds sidle. She likes to think that time passes. He infers the existence of an engine and a track. They're en route to Los Angeles when the collision occurs. But that was a special case. The hawk's dive is one fell swoop. Victims are designated "reactoids."

At the base of their neck, each wears the small scar of tenure. In public, wishing not to be conspicuous, they fold their wings, creating the image of a cape. The patient is the battery that runs the machines. Plurals are abstract, is abstract. A more difficult problem is the tail, which wants to twitch. In the heat of an explosion, body fluids boil. Dr. Davidson's tastes run to Latin flavors. So Thurber drew a fat example. In *Dallas*, capitalism and the family are the same thing, and no scene need last more than 90 seconds. I put in my thumb and you start to writhe. Bride, bridle, bridge. Dead leaves of a coleus. Between the towers the pilot and his mount glide smoothly, invisible to those on the ground but for what appears to be the reflection of the sun where no sun exists. In the distance the shadow of a man in the caboose waves slowly.

Seeing blown leaves, the toddler puckers. To understand is to "follow." Driven from the lips, tension gathers round the eye. A point of pride. He attempts a series of irrefutable *movements*. By style marked. Genghis Khan Antiques, Godfather's Restaurant. Years of carrying the heavy tray leave one shoulder lower than the other. I know now what I'd like to order. Am I also convinced that the earth exists? Protons, Pions, Dominions, Thrones. Above Fashion Valley they're building Fashion Hills. Minus continual impact the creature freezes. Twiddling shadows of late afternoon mix drowsiness with infinity's mystique.

Your paragraph. Pride is the plural. I put my tongue to the button. The mark of an attorney is contempt for the law. Theory is a place. Verbs never suit the frame. An angel named Mustang with blades of steel. Only part of the tree blows in the wind. Pistons contain the engagement. Cropped wide lawns and three models of homes to choose from. At this distance the skyline becomes sculpture. With the tower silent, each is left to his own devices, and some become human. As if being pulled through a tunnel toward a globe of light. In the ashtray, the cigarette burns to the filter.

You twist your key in the ignition. A woman mumbles and shakes. Fucking as if to stimulate an ideal reader. "A figure in white hovered at the end of this passage." So death-bed dreams are not incomparable. How am I supposed to feel? I mean: *licks* over those leaves. To master a branch of study. In dreams one floats from room to room. Dressed to match vinyl booths, the young waitress hums absently. Content seems increasingly prescribed. Michael heals. Uriel descends in a chariot of fire. Elsewise, do nothing.

from

Necromance

NECROMANCE

Poppy under a young
pepper tree, she thinks.
The Siren always sings
like this. Morbid
glamour of the singular.
Emphasizing correct names
as if making amends.

Ideal
republic of the separate
dust motes
afloat in abeyance.
Here the sullen
come to see their grudge
as pose, modeling.

The flame trees tip themselves
with flame.
But in that land
men prized
virginity. She washed
dishes in a black liquid
with islands of froth—
and sang.

Couples lounge
in slim fenced yards
beside the roar
of a freeway. Huge pine
a quarter mile off
floats. Hard to say where
this occurs.

Third dingy
bird-of-paradise
from right. Emphatic
precision
is revealed as
hostility. It is
just a bit further.

The mermaid's
privacy

CONTEXT

Clustered

berries at dusk
as possible

results. The chosen
contexts of display,

arrangement and arrival.

*

set against desultory or
"lonely"

puddles, drops.

*

Circles an old woman's
fingers trace
on the nubs of
her chair arms.

*

Waits for the word to come
to her, tensed
as if for orgasm.

Fear surrounds language.

THE GARDEN

Oleander: coral
from lipstick ads in the 50's.

Fruit of the tree of *such* knowledge.

To "smack"
(thin air)
meaning kiss or hit.

It appears
in the guise of outworn usages
because we are bad?

Big masculine threat,
insinuating and slangy.

SENSE

Twigs stiffen
the fingers.

Love of nature
is a translation.

Secret nodding
in the figurative:

a corroboration
which is taken for
"companion."

A saw warbles,
somewhere,
and the yards too
are terraced.

        *

Stress the birds lay
on that wire.

"*Possi*bly
holy parental emphases."

Big screen.

On the other side of
siding
cars go by.

String of fat
commas
as far as
we're concerned.

*

First the (non)sense
of direction.

"Stones to frogs,
then to princes
who do a circle dance
and turn to stone."

Good-night!

Meaning extends
her arm backward
ballerina-like:

wood-swirl
in the formica.

THE BOOK

There's a fly
holding its course, manfully,
several long seconds,
stolid as the old Buick.

I didn't jerk back
fast enough this time
and now I seem
to know what's coming next

as well as I do
my own mother
holding up the picture book.
This is the world

of objects, faking
an interest in their own affairs
long enough for me
(the child on the logo)

to feel comfortable
staring

ATTENTION

Ventriloquy
is the mother tongue.

Can you colonize rejection
by phrasing your request,

"Me want?"

Song: "I'm not a baby.
        Wa, Wa, Wa.

        I'm not a baby.
        Wa, Wa, Wa.

        I'm crazy
        like you."

The "you"
in the heart of
molecule and ridicule.

Marks resembling
the holes

in dead leaves
define the thing (moth wing).

That flutter
of indifference,

feigned?

But if lapses
are the dens

strategy aims
to conceal,

then you don't know
what you're asking.

LANGUAGE OF LOVE

There were distinctive
dips and shivers
in the various foliage,
syncopated,
almost cadenced in the way
that once made him invent
"understanding."

*

Now the boss could say
"parameters"
and mean something
like "I'll pinch."

By repeating the gesture exactly
the woman awakened
an excited suspicion
in the infant.

When he awakened
she was just returning from
one of her little trips.

It's common to confuse
the distance
with flirtation:
that expectant solemnity
which seems to invite a kiss.

He stroked her carapace
with his claw.
They had developed a code
in which each word appeared to refer
to some abdicated function.

Thus, in a department store,
Petite Impressions might neighbor
Town Square.

But he exaggerated it
by mincing
words like "micturition,"
setting scenes
in which the dainty lover
would pretend to leave.

*

Was it sadness or fear?
He still wasn't back.
The act of identification,
she recognized,
was *always* a pleasure,
but this lasting difference
between sense and recognition
made her unhappy

or afraid.
Once she was rewarded
by the beams
of headlights flitting
in play.

GETTING WARM

Tingle:
a shaft must be imagined to
connect the motes
though there is no light.

The notes.
If she's quiet
she's concentrating on the spaces
between cries, turning
times into spaces.

Is it memory or physics
that makes the bridge appear?
It looks nothing
like a real bridge.
She has to finish it
so it can explode.

She is in the dark,
sewing, stringing holes together
with invisible thread.
That's a feminine accomplishment:
a feat of memory, a managed
repletion or resplendence.

DISOWN

You may "have" sex—

but those round
sink-holes beneath
the off-ramps,

scabbed with whatever
flat, green stuff—

not in your most
nominative
moon-walk.

*

New one called
"Convoy Village."

Bylaws forbid
visible contrivance:

clotheslines
(like the skeleton)

or crabgrass
dead in long tracks
tipped with green.

Results shall be
unreminiscent.

*

To punch one's straw
definitely

into the fizz.

Arms of pastries
revolve
in their clear cylinder

slowly.

Space "may be shaped
like a saddle,"
scientists say.

A list may pantomime
focus.

On conditions
so numerous
nothing can begin.

*

"Run down," they say,
"buildings."

Wave of morning glory
leaves about to break
over the dropped plastic
bat, the empty shed.

Hard to specify
further.

Whole body
dotted

here and there

Areas of interest,

        cross purposes,

            eddies

from
Made to Seem

THE CREATION

Impressions
bribe or threaten
in order to live.

Retreating palisades
offer
a lasting
previousness.

*

Let us
move fast
enough, in a small
enough space, and
our travels
will take first
shape, then substance.

*

In the beginning
there was measurement.

How much
does self-scrutiny
resemble mother-touch?

*

Die Mommy scum!

To come true,
a thing must come second.

COVERS

The man
slapped her bottom
like a man did
in a video,

then he waited
as if for shadow
to completely cover the sun.

Moments later
archeologists found him.

*

The idea that they were reenacting something which had been
staged in the first place bothered her. If she wanted to go on,
she'd need to ignore this limp chronology. She assumed he was
conscious of the same constraint. But she almost always did
want to proceed. Procedure! If only either one of them believed
in the spontaneity of the original actors and could identify
with one. Be one. For this to work, she reasoned, one of us
would have to be gone.

*

"Well, look who missed
the fleeting moment,"

Green Giant gloats
over dazed children.

If to transpose
is to know,

we can cover our losses.

But only
If talking,

Formerly food,

Now meant
Not now

So recovery
Ran rings.

If to traverse
is to envelop,

I am held
and sung to sleep.

MY PROBLEM

It is my responsibility
to squeeze
the present from the past
by demanding particulars.

When the dog is used
to represent the inner
man, I need to ask,
"What kind of dog is it?"

If a parasitic
metaphor grows all
throughout—good!
Why stop with a barnacle?

A honeysuckle,
thrown like an arm
around a chain-link fence,
would be far more

articulated,
more precisely repetitive,
giving me the feeling
that I can go on like this

while the woman
at the next table says,
"You smell pretty,"

and sends her small daughter's
laugh, a spluttery orgasm,
into my ear—
though this may not have been
what you intended.

It may not be a problem
when I notice
the way the person shifts.

A PULSE

Find the place
in silence
that is a person

or like a person
or like not
needing a person.

*

After the heart attack
she fills her apartment
with designer accents—

piece by piece.

*

This is a bed,
an abiding
at least,

close to *lastly*
but nicer.

*

Light changes:

Separation
anxiety refers
to this

as next
tears itself off.

*

A hospital calendar
shows the sun going down
on an old-time,
round, lime-green
diner.

*

Just a quick trip back
to mark the spot
where things stop
looking familiar

NATIVE

How many constants *should* there be?

The slick wall of teeth?

The white stucco
at the corner,

flag on its porch
loosely snapping?

*

"Get to the point!"

as if before dark—

as if to some bench
near a four-way stop.

*

At what point does
dead reckoning's

net
replace the nest

and the body
of a parent?

*

The apparent
          present.

Here eucalyptus
leaves dandle,
redundant but syncopated.

CROSSING

We'll be careful.

Repression informs us
that this is not our father.

We distinguish
to penetrate.

We grow and grow,

fields of lilies,
cold funnels.

2

According to legend
Mom
sustains the universe
by yelling
"Stay there
where it's safe"
when every star
wants to run home
to her.

Now every single star
knows
she wants only
what's best
and winks steadily
to show it will obey,
and this winking
feels like the middle
of an interesting story.

This is where
our history begins.
Well, perhaps not
history, but we do
feel ourselves preceded.
(Homeostasis
means effortlessly
pursuing someone
who is just
disappearing.)

3
Now here it is
slowed down
by the introduction
of nouns.

Eastwood, Wayne
and Bogart:

faces
on a wall in Yuma

constitute
the force required
to resurrect
a sense of place.

(Hunger fits
like a bonnet
now, something
to distinguish.)

4

On the spot, our son
prefaced resorption, saying,

"You know how we're a lot alike . . ."

He couldn't go out
on that day, but
he could have a pickle.

Out of spite, he crawled
to the kitchen, demonstrating
the mechanics of desire.

5

The sky darkened
then. It seemed
like the wrong end
of a weak simile.
That was what shocked us.
None of our cries
had been heard,
but his was.
When something has happened
once, you might say

it's happened, "once and
for all." That's what
symbols mean
and why they're used
to cover up envy.

A STORY

Despite our infractions
we are loved
by the good mother
who speaks carefully:

"I love you, but I don't
like the way you lie there
pinching your nipples
while I'm trying to read you a story."

Once there was an old lady who told her son she
must go to the doctor because she was bleeding
down there. She didn't look alarmed, but suppressed
a smile, as if she were "tickled," as if she were
going to get away with something.

"Look," said the doctor, "you are confusing
infraction with profusion. *Despite*
may be divided into two
equal segments: Exceptional and Spiteful."

But the stubborn old woman just answered,
"When names perform a function,
that's fiction."

VISIBILITY

1

I have to go for a check-up. In the examining room I'm sur-
rounded by windows looking out on busy streets. The doctor
assures me these are one-way. In the dream, it is attractive to
be deceived.

2

Because of his name, I'm afraid this doctor's silences won't be
well-modulated. Motivated? The invisible barricades won't be
in the right places, and I won't be able to maneuver around
them, neatly, in the roadster I don't have—which is *supposed*
to be funny!

3

It's strange to see traffic backed up at this checkpoint—people
scattering—heading for the hills or darting across the freeway
toward the beach. There are words connected with this scene.
"Aliens" is one. If I can avoid these words, what remains
should be my experience.

THE DAFFODILS

Upon that inward eye

A wig and eyelashes
made of pipecleaners

affixed
to a rear view mirror

which says,
"Flapdoodle!"

in a common sense, country way
that just reflects

The bliss of solitude

and baby shoes
attached by a red tube

to the small plastic
blades of a "chopper":

this never-ending lineup
of spontaneous abortions

could have begun
as a singing crab

whose embarrassment
when brought before the king

was one way
to placate matter.

from Made to Seem　•　83

CONFIDENTIAL

Shooting pleasures
Ok'd by
My being seen
For
Or as
If.

*

Not just light
at the end of the tunnel,

but hearts, bows, rainbows—

all the stickers
teachers award if pleased.

* ∘

Pigeons bathe in technicolor
fluid "of a morning."

*

If I was banging
my head with a shoe,
I was just exaggerating—

like raising my voice
or the ante.

Curlicues
on iron gratings:

Can it be
a flourish is a grimace,
but a grimace isn't a flourish?

                 *

On the inscribed surface
of sleep.

Almost constant
bird soundings.

"Aloha, Fruity Pebbles!"

Music, useful
for abstracting emphasis.

Sweet nothing
to do with me.

LEAVING

The urge to wander is
displayed
in a spate of slick,
heart-shaped leaves.

*

Cellophane grass and
foil eggs.

The modesty

of standard presentation
does remind me of home
sickness.

*

As if some furtive
will's receded
leaving meaning
in its place:

A row of coastal
chalets

*

With waves
shine slides over
shine like skin's
what sections
same from same.

*

Coarse splay
of bamboo
from the gullies,
I write,
as if I'd been expecting
folds of lace.

*

Mine was about
escaping Death though
Death was stylized, somehow,
even stylish. So was I!
So I was hidden
among fashionable allies.

from
The Pretext

BIRTHMARK: THE PRETEXT

You want something; that's the pretext. I recently abandoned a dream narrative called "Mark." You can see it, since you asked.

MARK

I'm with three friends.
We've parked in a lot downtown,
lucky to get a slot.

My son's friend
asks him if he's divided
his homework in three parts;
luckily he has.

Suddenly, I'm the teacher.
I see a line of Milton's.
I'm glad I haven't marked it wrong;
at first I thought it didn't fit.

That's not very interesting or it's only interesting because it's real. It's a real dream composed of three banal vignettes in which the same elements appear: luck, parts, and fit. It's interesting to the extent that the divisions and the fitting together arise spontaneously, without pretext. In other words, to the extent that there is a stranger in my head arranging things for me. Of course, I divided the *poem* in three parts. I chose the word *lucky*.

I have a real birthmark: a large red one on my outer left thigh. When I was a child, my mother referred to it as a "strawberry mark," with seeming affection. Was that some kind of trick? Because of what she called it, the mark has never troubled me.

I didn't mind having small breasts either, though in that case there *were* negative terms attached. Flat-chested, etc. But gender is the birthmark which has bothered me. When I was a child, Marilyn Monroe was the Sex Queen. I know people feel kindly toward "Marilyn," but I saw something horrific in her act. Brilliantly horrific, maybe. She turned a magnifying glass on the problem. Those unwieldy bosoms held together by the weak "spaghetti straps." Tee-hee. Something was inadequate. The squeaky little girl voice would never be able to articulate all that matter. No mind could get around it. So she would be a stranger to herself (and what could be more embarrassing or exciting)? Was someone ever lucky! We watched her pretend to pretend to be transfixed in the highbeams of our little girl stare. Funny how you can be excited without fitting in anywhere. But I've gone off on a tangent when what I wanted to do was swallow my own pretext.

WRITING

The clerk half skips away in his jaunty-officious hurry. Oh, he's telling me a joke about our common inability to occupy two planes. What he can't know is that I hate body language. "My life had stood, a little speech, a clipped coupon." Hell is unredeemed experience?

If I were dying in a hospital bed, would I get pencil and paper to jot down passing thoughts? Not likely. I, myself, was always a forwarding address.

But here's the joke: syntactic space predates and dominates these words.

>We must take reasoning tests
>before passing
>through a cut-out
>arabesque
>in the Islamic
>facade beyond which
>small boats wait
>to carry us
>to the icebergs.
>We hunker down
>with short pencils
>in front of the ticket booth.

ARTICULATION

I

With whom
do you leave yourself
during reveries?

The one making coffee
or doing the driving—

that is the real
person in your life.
Now that one is gone

or has tagged along with you
like a small child
behind Mother.

"No!" you explain
in the crowded aisle.

"Without articulation
there's *no* sense of place."

2

When I dreamed about flying,
it was as a skill
I needed to regain.

I'd make practice runs
and float high
over the page. Pleasure

was a confirmation.
I remembered the way
and I was right!

Still,
one should be patient

with the present
as if with a child.

To follow its prattle—
glitter on water—

indulgently
is only polite.

NEAR RHYME

Do I regret *each* thing
I recall?
Or regret remembering
anything uncalled for

and wrapping it up
as if as
a gift?

I resent believing
there is someone else present
while I think there isn't.

*

That young girl listening
to "Angel Baby"

on a pink plastic radio
while staring out her window
at the planet Venus

was conscious
of doing what girls do—

thrilled to correspond.

That is what it means
to be young.

I could make you want it:
The protein carousel,
pronouns.

So what if
self is
else played backwards?

                    *

He rhymes
the disparate

nuclei, each one
bow-tie on

"nothing really"

QUALIA

Pole's shadow qualifies
asphalt
in its measured manner.

Where impact
has become tenor, that's
the length of time.

The redness
of red,

the sad way light
whitesides the tops of stems.

Duration, for instance,
is eerie.

And there can be
clear arrhythmias—

A wind-chime singly,
then a fluttering

faster than the heart
is such a tease.

You think you know them,

need to stay
where they're going.

MY ASSOCIATES

You identify
with the body's
routine

until you think
it's your body—

like thinking
you *are* the clock.

Identity is a form
of prayer.

"How do I look?"

meaning what
could I pass for

where every eye's
a guard.

May passes
as the whole
air's bedizened
flotilla.

To echo
is to hold
aloft?

Then take any word
and split it,

make it soil itself
to seem fertile.

So nasturtiums
are the dirt's
lips.

Fecund. Cunning. (Cunt)

GREETING

That wood pole's
rosy crossbar,

shouldering a complement
of knobs,

like clothespins
or Xmas lights,

to which crinkly
wires rise up
from adjacent yards.

*

I miss *circumstance*
already—

the way a single word
could mean

necessary, relative,
provisional

and a bird flicks past
leaving

the sense that one
has waved one's hand.

SETS

Scheduled:
a two part
investigation

Recalling
the investigation

*

These bi
furcated
ovals
stand up
from the clear red stems—

not like hairs,
not like soldiers—

in this quietness.

*

Time's tic:
to pitch forward
then catch "itself"
again.

"We're" bombing Iraq again.

If I turn on the news,
someone will say, "We
mean business."

*

Eyes open wide
to form

an apology?
Disguised as what
might be surprise

over the raised
spoon.

ABOUT

What's the worst that could happen?

"Schools of fish are trapped
In these pools,"
Say the anchors

Who hang
On nursing home walls.

Reference is inimical,
We find out now;

Its Moebius strip
Search called

Vital
To security.

Just keep moving
And it's about a snake.

About how long

Should we be able
To recoil? Recall?

Our brothers
Were already changed

Into enormous birds
    like those.

We're the target audience.

Both male and female
Woodstorks wade.

THE PLOT

The secret is
you can't get to sleep
with a quiet mind;
you need to follow a sentence,
inward or downward,
as it becomes circuitous,
path-like, with tenuously credible
foliage on either side of it—
but you're still not sleeping.
You're conscious of the metaphoric
contraption; it's too jerky,
too equivocal to suspend you

And Nature was the girl who could spin
babies out of dustballs
until that little man
who said he had a name showed up
and wanted them
or wanted to be one
of a cast of cartoon
characters assigned to manage
the Garden
so even Adam and Eve discovered
they somehow *knew* the punchline:
the snake would swallow
the red bomb

Why is sleep's border guarded?
On the monitors
professional false selves
make self-disparaging remarks.
There's a sexy bored housewife,
very Natalie Wood-like,
sighing, "Men should win"—
but the only thing that matters
is the pace of substitution.
You feel like trying to escape
from her straight-arrow husband
and her biker boyfriend

You can't believe
you're on Penelope's Secret.
A suitor waits
for ages
to be hypnotized
on stage.

HERE

1

I'm here to recreate
the "fleeting impression"
that others once saw themselves

as repositories of experience.
In a dream,
I'm three old actors

known for playing in Westerns.
We're on a trek through wild country
to show how the past might have been.

A voice-over says that our saddles
are especially worn and rough-hewn.

2

It's supposed to be beautiful
to repeat a motif
in another medium.

A regular
dither
in the strings

approaching Apollo
Cremation. Out front,
fountains

make a statement
about the ability
to keep up one's end.

There's a boy down the street,
firing caps
as my son did

while a church plays
its booming
recording of chimes.

OVER

Roused, you ask, "Wasn't that . . .?"

A breath, a stitch,
a harpoon.

You throw like a girl!

LIGHT

Not with an order but a question,
apropos of nothing.

Something answers "Dark" and "Light."

These two
new beings are startled and draw back

from the beginning of time.
Are you happy?

*

No exit but attenuation?

Sky barely
orange at sunset.

Pulled out slow and thin,
her voice

means an objection
so pervasive
cannot know its enemy.

*

The purpose of abstraction
is to discover how
two things
can constitute a recurrence.

To obtain reversibility.
Gravity is to memory . . .

from The Pretext • 111

STATEMENT

In my country
facts are dead children.

When I say "dissociation,"
I may have said "real-time action."

This is my given name:

Thirty-One Year Old
Prima-Gravida,

The Pokey-Puppy.

Words
can be repeated.

The Distractible Sparrow,
The Smallest District.

The Strictest Definition.

Astronomers know
a signal's
not an answer.

Veil

FALLING: 1

The snake was damned
because he filled

his own wake
everywhere,

obviating body-
            image.

To swallow your own tail—

or tale
is no longer

an approved
form of transportation.

A human
fiddles with the yes/no
switch,

the new/old
binary

exhibitionism.

Go ahead,
        say anything.

FALLING: 2

You may have a hoof
in two worlds,

but you can't confess,
for then you wouldn't

be at risk
of public exposure

and it is exactly
your relation to exposure
which comprises your act.

The precipice
over which you might slip
deliberately placed there,

almost a joke now,
shared with the audience

who are left
holding what appears to be
one edge.

Complicity is the real
subject. An invisible

wink in a void?
A familiarity that threatens

to melt
into uniform poignance.

What we remember best
about you

is the quality
of your anticipation

THEORIES

Bird calls rise
and drop
to an unseen floor.

The son pretends
to slip
and falls

into a wading
pool,

limbs frozen
akimbo,
eyes locked

on mother.
One person

stutters as a way of
insisting
on unconditional love

and one who hears
a busy signal
may ring again

in anger.
What if one pretends

to restrain another
while the other

seems
to rotate helplessly

faster
and faster?

Each finds
his mate pre-

dictable

but believes his own
rigidity

must excite
his partner

AS WE'RE TOLD

At the start, something must be arbitrarily excluded.
The saline solution. Call it an apple. Call this a test
or a joke. From now on, apple will mean arbitrary
choice or "at random." Any fence maintains the other
side is "without form." When we're thrown out, it's onto
the lap of our parent. Later, though, Mother puts
the apple into Snow White's hand,
and then it's poison!

SYSTEMIC

What the pulse flushes.

Research indicates
that the shift

from cars to trucks
reflects a desire

for solid
conviction.

Day breaks.
Dog's bark shoots

through the soles of my feet
to my crotch.

*

There *was* light
and I was trying to catch up,

to understand what had happened
retrospectively

by barking
appropriate commands.

This season
frozen hoopla

will ornament
exchanges.

Calls to worship
disposable stand-ins

appear
in every hand.

OVERHEARING

The way "The Tennessee Waltz"
is about having heard

"The Tennessee Waltz"
before:

an almost floral
nostalgia,

totally self-
contained,

is what we call
beautiful.

                    *

You're in the rocker;
I'm on the couch,
long since hauled off, but
stationed
like organs
in this dream.

You're saying,
a bit too loudly,
so that I'm afraid
the one doing dishes
(now dead)
and the one in the bathroom
(now gone)

will overhear,
why you first wanted me,

when I wake up
to hear you
thrashing,
yelling out in a dream

THE WAY

Card in pew pocket
announces,
"I am here."

I made only one statement
because of a bad winter.

Grease is the word; grease
is the way

I am feeling.
Real life emergencies or

flubbing behind the scenes.

As a child,
I was abandoned

in a story
made of trees.

Here's the small
gasp

of this clearing
come "upon" "again"

ONGOING

Some cartoon kids
watch cartoons

on a tiny
black-and-white tv

where a sit-com cartoon
couple from the fifties

approach a door
on which a sign reads,

"Don't exist!"

*

The trick is to
dissolve

my gaze

midway between
warning and appeal.

When I'm metaphorical,
I'm happy.

When an effort
was a small engine,

then I loved it
like a mommy.

*

Room alive
with ambient

recapitulation.

Random firing
in my sleep

to balance out
experience,

corporate-funded
homunculi

in an infinite
regress

PIECEMEAL

A boy severs his fingers,
by accident, in my imagination

where his first thought is

"My mother
will be so frightened!"

                    *

Horn jags
from a stereo

as evasive
maneuvers:

extruded ink
jets, sea snakes

turn mouth-forward,
bodies snapping

as if

out of sight,
as if

*

over and over

were a scouting party
that arrives,

piecemeal,

in the third
person

REHEARSAL

The characters are sounds made by various sizes and kinds of engines. They continue to enter indefinitely, in random order, but are always recognized. Each mentions respiration as something that has already occurred.

*

Is a short time
circular?

Practiced?

Loops
on ruled paper.

What is supervised
has meaning.

A brow-beating
pulse

VEIL

The doll told me
to exist.

It said, "Hypnotize yourself."

It said time would be
transfixed.

*

Now the optimist

sees an oak
shiver

and a girl whiz by
on a bicycle

with a sense of pleasurable
suspense.

She budgets herself
with leafy

prestidigitation.

I too
am a segmentalist.

*

But I've dropped
more than an armful

of groceries or books

downstairs
into a train station.

An acquaintance says
she colors her hair

so people will help her
when this happens.

To refute her argument,
I must wake up

and remember my hair's
already dyed.

*

As a mentalist,
I must suffer

lapses

then repeat myself
in a blind trial.

I must write
punchlines only I
can hear

and only after
I've passed on

WHOLE

Under the skin,
it's as if a woman
is fastening
five more flashlights
to the handlebars
of her bicycle.

*

A man decorates
his cap with phrases
glued to big buttons—

one of them
says, "Split."

*

And we've hung up glass balls,
making points of light,

where the point is
to *have been* multiplied.

*

If to count
is to recount

what's missing . . .

*

One's conviction
that she is in the wrong
hospital bed
or room
or that this is not
a room
at all, that this
is not a hospital.

*

The flock veers
and its form
catches up with it.

When body was wild
posturing, what would
imposture have been?

OUR NATURE

The very flatness
of portraits
makes for nostalgia
in the connoisseur.

Here's the latest
little lip of wave
to flatten
and spread thin.

Let's say
it shows our recklessness,

our fast gun,

our self-consciousness
which was really

our infatuation
with our own fame,

our escapes,

the easy way
we'd blend in

with the peasantry,

our loyalty
to our old gang

from among whom
it was our nature

to be singled out

MANUFACTURING

1

A career in vestige management.

A dream job
back-engineering
shifts in salience.

I'm so far
behind the curve
on this.

So. Cal.
must connect with
so-called

to manufacture
the present.

Ubiquity's
the new in-joke

bar-code hard-on,

a catch-phrase
in every segment.

2

The eye asks if the green,

frilled geranium puckers,
clustered at angles

on each stem,
are similar enough

to stop time.

It has asked this question already.

How much present tense
can any resemblance make?

What if one catch-phrase
appears in every episode?

Does the language go rigid?

The new in-joke
is a pun
pretending to be a bridge.

THE PLAN

"Who told you
you were visible?"

God said,

meaning naked
or powerless.

*

We had planned this meeting
in advance,

how we'd address each other,

how we'd stand
or kneel.

Thus our intentions
are different

from our bodies,
something extra,

though transparent
like a negligee.

*

Though a bit sketchy,

like this palm's
impression of a tree—

flashing scales,

on the point of
retraction.

But *sweet.*
You don't understand!

Like a lariat made of scalloped bricks

circling a patch
of grass

COUNTER

"Endless" meaning soul

or soulless.

*

Flower buckets
with the goose logo

at either end
of a sentence.

*

A waitress asks whether
my soup is good

   and winks

as if only she and I know
what "good" means.

WORDS

Click here
to express your view

of the continuing
unrest.

"I think he's hiding
behind a screen

of words

and I think that's
very dangerous."

The caller says, "Please
rate these words

in the order
of their importance."

"On the issue of
what this issue
is about,"

on my voodoo self-
reference, which

has to be groundless,

which, in order to impress,
must come

from the blue
thinking cap of sky

into which pines
disgorge large birds

INSIDE OUT

Since you're exasperated,
you may be a tycoon

exasperated by the stupidity
of the little man.

You may have your own tv show
and not know it.

You say:

It's a set-up from the crib out.

Mind is a conspiracy
so we're being watched.

There are shadowy forces
around this build-up

to the standing
wave
of the present

(to the desire for acclaim).

*

What if God's only message
is "Repeat after me?"

This tireless yodel.

This make-work program

These bright cloud
bridges to nowhere
with their thankless
symmetrically frayed edges.

That woman in the street
wailing "Fucker!"
as she passes
out of range

PURPOSE

From the first
abstraction,

loss
is edible.

To think
is to filter

passers-by through your
semi-permeable membrane;

keep yourself
in circulation.

What if appetite
is a by-product?

If you pass through
zero,

you may see someone
you love.

Here's your mother
with her anxious grasp,

her clock-watching

About the author

Rae Armantrout is Adjunct Professor of literature at University of California, San Diego, and the author of six books of poetry, most recently *Made to Seem* (Sun & Moon, 1995). Her work has been published in numerous anthologies, including *Poems for the Millennium* edited by Pierre Joris and Jerome Rothenberg (University of California Press, 1997), *Postmodern American Poetry: A Norton Anthology* edited by Paul Hoover (Norton, 1994), *Best American Poetry of 1988* edited by John Ashbery (Scribners, 1989), *Language Poetries* edited by Douglas Messerli (New Directions, 1987) and *In the American Tree* edited by Ron Silliman (National Poetry Foundation, 1986). One of her poems from *Veil*, "The Plan," has been chosen by Robert Hass to be included in *Best American Poetry of 2001*, forthcoming.

DATE DUE

DEC 0 6 2002			
GAYLORD			PRINTED IN U.S.A.